Interview with a PANDA

& Other Endangered Animals Too

Written by
Andy Seed

Illustrated by
Nick East

WELBECK

Published in 2023 by Welbeck Children's Books
An imprint of Welbeck Children's Limited, part of Welbeck Publishing Group.
Offices in: London - 20 Mortimer Street, London W1T 3JW &
Sydney - Level 17, 207 Kent St, Sydney NSW 2000 Australia
www.welbeckpublishing.com

Designer: Sam James
Senior Editor: Jenni Lazell

FSC
www.fsc.org
MIX
Paper | Supporting
responsible forestry
FSC® C020056

ISBN 978-1-80453-508-0

Printed in Heshan, China

10 9 8 7 6 5 4 3 2 1

Contents

Introduction

Ever since I invented my wacky and wondrous TRANIMALATOR, a machine that allows me to TALK to ANIMALS, I have had a totally good time meeting the world's wildlife. For this book I decided to speak to REALLY RARE creatures. Why? Because it might be the last chance to do that. EEK!

Yes, it's COMPLETE POOP that lots of Earth's animals are endangered. They are at risk of dying out, and we need to help them. I decided that a good start would be to interview some of these beasts and see what they have to say. You can read their words RIGHT HERE.

I was actually flabbergasted at how many different kinds of animals are close to horrible EXTINCTION. I mean, I talked to a cuddly panda, a terrifying croc, an enormous elephant, a tiny toad, a gorgeous flying fox, and even something hairy called a kākāpō. Not bad, huh?

JUST SAY, "NO COMMENT!"

It wasn't easy, oh no. I mean, most of these species are not happy with us humans. They are REALLY ANGRY. Some of them are so TOTALLY BALLISTIC that I had to be MR. SORRY most of the time. In fact, I'm probably now the world's best apologizer. The good thing is that this book does include a section about HOW YOU CAN HELP endangered animals. In the meantime, enjoy discovering what they have to say!

Interview with a
Giant Panda

I am SO excited about this interview! Here is
one of the most ADORABLE animals in the
WHOLE WORLD. I give you the gorgeous, cuddly,
and really quite large ... GIANT PANDA!

Q: It's taken ages to find you—why do you live here in these remote mountains in China?
A: We like a quiet life *MUNCH MUNCH*. Imagine if I lived in a town, *MUNCH*, I'd never get any peace. Life would totally CHEW.

Q: You mean bite?
A: Yes, that.

Q: So what do you do all day? What do pandas get up to? Do you have any hobbies?
A: *MUNCH*. Hobbies? Not really. *MUNCH MUNCH MUNCH*.

Q: What about, um, eating? You do seem to eat a lot.
A: *MUNCH MUNCH* and what makes *MUNCH* you *MUNCH* say that? *MUNCH*.

Q: Oh, just a munch—I mean hunch. What exactly is the stuff you're stuffing into your face?
A: *MUNCH* this? *MUNCH* this *MUNCH* is *MUNCH* bam *MUNCH* boo.

Q: Bamboo! Do you mean those wooden poles that people use for gardening?
A: *MUNCH* yes. I mean no. *MUNCH* it's the same plant, but we eat them when they are soft and green, not woody. We munch the leaves and the shoots *MUNCH*. I think that's enough now, *BURP!*

Q: What, a great big bear like you just eats salad? How does that give you enough energy?
A: It doesn't. I mean it does, but not much. That's why we sleep and rest a lot—to save energy. And it's why we poop about 40 times a day. Lots of fiber! *YAWN*.

Q: Right . . . I found a book in the library that said there are not many pandas left in the wild. Why are there not more of you?
A: More of me? *YAWN* there's only one of me, of course . . . OH, I SEE! Yes, well, pandas have been endangered, it's true, and it's all YOUR FAULT. I don't mean you are to blame, I mean all of you: HUMAN PEOPLE BEINGS.

Q: *Gulp,* what did we do?

A: Oh, not much, I mean you only took away our forests, our food, our land, our peace, our space, our safety, our *YAWN,* I mean our habitat. Human people here in Asia cut down so many trees, they turned our forests into farmland and built roads and railroads. We had to go into the hills, but we can't live squashed together—we need space! They did worse things, too.

Q: Oh dear, like what?

A: Like hunted us. Killed us for food and for our warm fur, and captured us alive to be put in cages and stared at all day.

Q: Sorry. I'll add you to the list of animals that I need to apologize to, big time. So, um, it sounds like you don't like zoos either?

A: How would you like to *YAWN* be kept behind bars all day?

Q: But zoos have helped breed pandas so that you're not endangered any more—did you know that?

A: I know that pandas don't like breeding in zoos. Would you like to raise a family in prison? I mean *YAWWN* we don't even have many kids out here in the WILD.

Q: Why's that?

A: *YAWWWWWWN* well, females like me, we live alone and only meet up with a fella to mate for a couple of days a year usually. Then our babies are teeny-weeny-pinky-blindy little things. It's a wonder they survive at all! We have to watch out for leopards and *YAWN* eagles too.

Q: Some bears hibernate. Do you?

A: *YAWNO*. I mean no.

Q: OK, got that. Finally, is there anything you'd like to tell the readers?

A: Yes.

Q: Um, what is it?

A: Be nice, be kind *YAWN*. Or I'll bite you on the bum! *ZZZZzzzz . . .*

Interview with a
Sumatran Elephant

Next is a BIG interview with a BIG BEAST from
Indonesia. Ten feet tall, weighing four tons
and with 60,000 muscles in his ENORMOUS
nose, I present a SUMATRAN ELEPHANT!

Q: What's it like being so HUGE?
A: Am I huge or are you small? Whales are bigger than me.
Giraffes taller, some snakes longer. It is the MIND that counts,
not the body, O breaker.

**Q: Ah, I couldn't agree more. But my name is Andy,
so why do you call me breaker?**
A: You are a man, and men are breakers. Your kind has
broken this island.

**Q: Oh dear. You mean Sumatra, where we are?
I didn't break it, honest.**
A: Sumatra, as you call it, is one of the world's largest islands.
It was once home to many types of creature: fierce tiger, mighty
rhino, gentle orangutan, and many tribes of strong elephant.
But our lands have been taken, broken from us. All are
dying out.

Q: I see. So what kind of land do you need to live?
A: We are dwellers of the tropical woods. Much of
the island was once covered in rich rainforest. It was
full of plants and fruit for us to eat. We eat a LOT,
so we need to move around all the time.

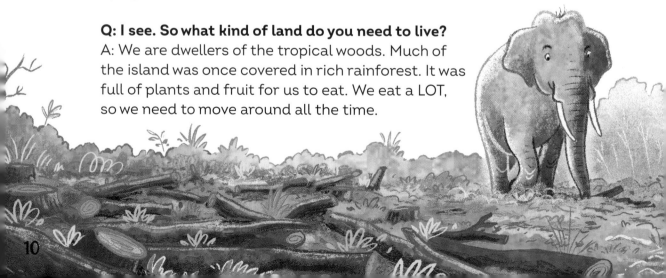

Q: What has happened to the forests then?
A: Breakers cut them down. They have destroyed the trees that hold the life of the island together. Stolen them to make farmland or build houses or plant bushes that do not belong here.

Q: I read that Sumatran elephants are in danger of going extinct—is this why?
A: It is part of the reason. Breakers also kill us for our ivory tusks. Others poison us to keep us from eating their crops. We do not want to be near humans, but we have to move around to survive.

Q: You mean to find enough food?
A: It is not just that. We have traditional migration routes around the island—ways we have walked for thousands of years. By following these we meet other herds of elephants and find partners to mate with. If we do not have babies, we do not survive.

11

Q: This is all very sad. Is there anything good you can tell the readers?
A: Of course. You are not all breakers. And we understand that the humans who live here need land too. Some wise people have made national parks, where we are protected from poachers and loggers. No one can cut down the trees in them.

Q: Will the national parks help you survive?
A: They might, but they need to be REALLY BIG so they can support many herds of elephants.

Q: Hopefully, this book will help kids understand your problems, then perhaps when they grow up, they might not become, uh, breakers. So,can you tell us some more interesting facts about Sumatran elephants?
A: We can't jump.

Q: Right . . . um, anything else?
A: Yes. Our poop is REALLY BIG because we eat for about 16 hours a day. And that is GOOD because our plops help spread seeds around the island so that the forests grow a good mix of plants.

Q: Nice! And what do you use your trunk for?
A: MANY things! I use mine to breathe, to eat, to reach and grab things, to drink, to wash by spraying water or dust, to touch, to make trumpeting noises, and to WHACK anything that annoys me.

**Q: Wow, I wish my nose could do all that!
And what about your tusks?**
A: They are special teeth used for lots of jobs like digging for salt, scratching trees to mark my territory, showing off to girls, and they are handy if I have to fight any TROUBLESOME elephants.

Q: Do you often have fights?
A: No, THANK GOODNESS.

**Q: OK and lastly—is there anything you'd
like to say to the readers?**
A: Please help us survive. Don't be a breaker.

**Wise advice. Thank you
for the interview!**

Interview with a
Kākāpō

I'm now on an island covered in forests, just off the coast of New Zealand. In front of me is a big, green, blotchy creature, one of the world's rarest and most unusual birds. It's EXCITING!

Q: How are you today, Mrs. Kākāpō?
A: Not bad, fella, not bad. So whatcha wanna know?

Q: You look like a well-built parrot. Or are you a green owl?
A: Haha, lots of people say that. I'm a parrot but I can't fly.

Q: Why not?
A: Too heavy, mate. And I got titchy wings, see.

Q: So how did you get into that tree?
A: I can't fly, but I'm not bad at climbing. Strong claws, see. Gotta climb to reach food, you know.

Q: Oh right, so what do you eat?
A: Fruit and seeds mainly, with a few juicy leaves now and then. We're veggies, mate.

Q: Wait, WHAT WAS THAT NOISE?
A: Oh, that was a male. They make a loud mating call called "booming" for about seven hours EVERY NIGHT. Does my head in . . .

Q: And can I ask, uh, why do you have, um, a hairy face?
A: I am NOT HAIRY. The nerve! Those are special feathers around my beak. It helps me feel my way around in the dark.

Q: But aren't you asleep when it's dark?
A: No, mate. We're NOCTURNAL. We mainly roost in the day and then come out at night when it's safer, you know.

Q: Ah, maybe that's why you look a bit like an owl ... Anyway, what are you keeping safe from? I can't see any predators on this island.
A: Well, there are big eagles around sometimes—that's when our green, mottled camouflage helps. And my dad told me there used to be nasty cats and rats and stoats that ate a lot of kākāpōs, especially the chicks in nests on the ground. Easy prey.

Q: Oh, is that why kākāpō are endangered?
A: One of the reasons, mate. Long ago the native Māori people hunted us with dogs, too. But then a bunch of twits showed up in New Zealand and brought cats and stoats and ferrets here. Those predators found us easy to catch 'cause we can't fly away.

Q: Which twits would do a silly thing like THAT?
A: They looked a bit like you, mate. Settlers from Europe. They came in boats long ago and started cutting down our forests to make farmland. So we had fewer places to live, you know. There used to be thousands of us, but by the 1990s there were only 51 kākāpō in all of New Zealand. Fella, we almost DIED OUT.

Q: Yikes. I am REALLY sorry. Lucky that you found this island with no predators, isn't it?
A: Haha, not really.

Q: What do you mean?
A: My parents were brought here over 10 years ago by NICE PEOPLE. The government wanted to save us, so they set up the AWESOME Kākāpō Recovery Programme in '95. They cleared all the rats, cats, and stoats off a few islands and then brought us here, making sure there's plenty of food. It's FABBO!

Q: Whew, I'm glad that we humans have helped you in the end. So what's that tag around your leg?
A: Oh every kākāpō is tagged, and we even have radio transmitters so the rangers can monitor us. They care for eggs and chicks—mate, they even FEED us sometimes! Our numbers are recovering slowly too: there are about 200 of us now!

Q: That's, uh, fabbo. Hey is that your name on the tag?
A: Uh, dunno mate, I can't read. What does it say?

Q: It says your name is Waa. Is that right?
A: Waa? WAA! My name is Doris!

Whoops, awkward. I guess they needed a tranimalator ... bye, uh, Doris.

Interview with a
Cuban Crocodile

Nervous? Me? No, no way, not at all. I mean,
I am face to face with the most aggressive
crocodile in the world, that's all. HELP!

Q: Hello, nice Mr. Crocodile, how are you today?
A: How generous of you to ask. I am indeed well. And may I
just say what an honor it is to be included in your splendid
animal Q&A series. Thank you for inviting me.

**Q: Ah, well, it's a pleasure. Are all crocodiles as polite
as you?**
A: Oh no, no, no, not by any means. Alligators are rude,
caimans loud and smelly, and gharials have no manners
at all. And saltwater crocodiles eat with their mouths
open. Revolting.

**Q: So what makes you different from those others you
mention, besides, uh, manners?**
A: Excellent question, if I might say so, well done.
Well, sir, we are small—usually six to ten feet long—
we walk high and proud on our long, strong, legs,
and we are rather speedy.

Q: Do all of you live in swamps like this?
A: Sorry, I beg your pardon—could you repeat that, please?

Q: Is this where all Cuban crocs live?
A: Ah, right, I think I heard that right. Indeed, we are marsh dwellers. We inhabit freshwater wetlands as well as rivers. But we spend a lot of time on land too.

Q: And what do you eat?
A: I, um, think I heard that question. My sincere apologies, I really am hard of hearing. Perhaps, if you would be so kind, you could come a little closer to help me?

Q: OK, is that better? Your favorite foods are . . . ?
A: Most kind, that is a little easier. Right, well, we catch turtles, fish, and sometimes shellfish like shrimp too. But my preference is to snap a rat or bird from the branches of a tree.

Q: Wow, how do you do that?
A: I *think* I heard what you said. Well, we can leap up from the water with a swish of our big, strong tails, see.

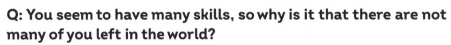

Q: You seem to have many skills, so why is it that there are not many of you left in the world?
A: Oh dear, that was so difficult for me to hear. Please do step closer so I can understand. I would be, um, very grateful...

Q: Wait, I know, I'll just turn up the volume on the tranimalator. There, how's that?
A: Oh can't you just come CLOSER? For goodness sake, come on—it won't hurt!

Q: I, um, think I might just stay here... You can hear, can't you?
A: OF COURSE I CAN HEAR YOUR STUPID QUESTIONS! Gah, you humans are just SO ANNOYING! And you taste SO NICE!

Q: Gulp. You've eaten people?
A: No, but I was hoping to... Anyway, you deserve it—it was YOU PEOPLE who made us endangered! Years ago there were Cuban crocodiles all over the Caribbean. Now there's just a measly little group of us left in this swamp! GRRRR!

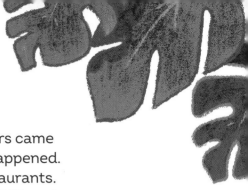

Q: What happened?

A: What happened? WHAT HAPPENED? Hunters came with guns and nets and killed us, that's what happened. My friends and family have been EATEN in restaurants. Some of my cousins had their skin sold for SHOES and BAGS. Not exactly nice, is it? No wonder I am FURIOUS!

Q: But I have heard that there is a special plan going on here in Cuba to save you. And zoos are breeding baby crocs to release back into the wild. Did you know that?

A: So let me get this straight. Humans are working hard to produce more Cuban crocodiles? Well, would it not be easier just to STOP SHOOTING US?

Q: That's a good point. I think it's different people doing the two things. Is it OK if I go now?

A: Yes, and NEVER COME BACK! Unless I can eat you.

COME BACK, I'M LONLEY. AND HUNGRY!

Interview with a
Black Rhino

Next up is a BIG, bulky beast from Zambia, in Africa. She weighs a ton and looks like she won't take any sass, so I'd better be REAL CAREFUL. Yes, here I am chatting with a BLACK RHINO!

Q: Um, gulp, hello, Ms. Rhino, would you, uh, mind at all if I asked you, uh, a few questions?
A: YES! Now GO AWAY or I'll charge and squash you flatter than a POSTAGE STAMP.

Q: Oh dear, sorry, well that was a short interview...
A: HAHA, got you! ONLY KIDDING! Of course I'll answer your questions. I LOVE interviews!

Q: Really?
A: Sure! A lot of people think we are grumpy and dangerous all the time, but we're only like that if we feel THREATENED, and you look like you couldn't hurt a baby slug.

Q: Whew! Speaking of babies, is that little one yours?
A: Yes, isn't he GORGEOUS. He was born a week ago, a bouncing 105 pounds, and his name is Ken.

Q: Ah, sweet. Hello, Ken. Um, why doesn't he have a horn like you?
A: It hasn't grown yet. Eventually he'll grow two horns, one big and one small, like mine. Because he's a male, the horn could be up to THREE FEET long!

Q: What are your horns for?
A: Honking at traffic, of course.

Q: What?
A: HAHA, I do like jokes . . . No, we use them to defend ourselves– mainly against other rhinos–and to help find food by breaking off branches or digging around.

Q: So do rhinos FIGHT each other?
A: You bet, fella! Of course, it's mainly the MALES. They sometimes compete over us girls, you know? Sometimes they suffer really bad injuries and DIE. Honestly, I know I am STUNNING, but no need to go THAT far . . .

23

Q: Right, uh, you mentioned food just then. What do rhinos eat?

A: Lions, crocodiles, hyenas mainly . . . NOT REALLY hehe, just kidding again. No, we are herbitarians, um I mean vegevores, you know PLANT EATERS. We chomp leaves and bushy stuff. No, the lions, crocs, and hyenas try and eat us—well, our babies. That's why Ken stays very close to me!

Q: Are there any predators that hunt adult rhinos?

A: Huh, I'd like to see them TRY. I weigh over 2,200 pounds and can blast along at over 30 miles per hour when I'm in a fury. They will either get SMASHED or end up with a horn up the butt!

Q: Nice! Are you the BOSS of this part of Africa, then?

A: NO. Annoyingly, there's something bigger and heavier that wants the same food as us. Elephants. I'm not going to argue with THEM.

Q: Right, fair enough. By the way, why are you called a black rhino when you are gray?

A: I have NO IDEA. White rhinos are gray too. CRAZY, isn't it?

Q: Hmmm. Now, I don't really want to ask this, but what do you think of *people?*

A: Some are OK, like you, and most of the tourists that just want a photo. Also, the park rangers that take care of us are brill. But some humans I want to BASH to PIECES.

Q: Oh dear, who are they?
A: They're called POACHERS, and they have nearly WIPED US OUT. They carry guns and they shoot us, then saw off our horns to sell. I've heard rhino rumors that HORRIBLE humans make the horns into medicines (which don't work) and dagger handles. DUH!

Q: I agree they are horrible and I am sorry that you are endangered. Most of us want to protect you.
A: I know. Excuse me while I pee on this tree.

Q: OK, uh, why are you doing that?
A: It's to let other rhinos know I'm around, so we can maybe get together for a chat tonight when it's cooler. Our sense of smell, like our hearing, is totally mega, you know.

Q: And finally, how do I tell a white rhino from a black rhino?
A: They have an ENORMOUS W across their head. Haha, just kidding AGAIN. No, they are bigger and have different shaped lips. Ours are better.

Right, time to go. I hope this interview was free—I don't want you to CHARGE ...

Interview with a
Green Turtle

Now I am at the beach in sunny Mexico, about to interview a huge reptile, over three feet long! She has a shell, flippers, and quite a grumpy face: meet a GREEN SEA TURTLE!

Q: It's nice to chat here on the beach—are you on vacation?
A: Turtles don't have vacations. Can you move, please—you're in the way.

Q: Oh, sorry. So you're doing some good digging. Um, are you making a sandcastle?
A: A what? Look, just stand back, will you? I'm digging a nest.

Q: A nest? On a beach? Are you sure?
A: I'm sure you're annoying! And tuck your shirt in—you look like a mess. I'm going to lay 100 eggs here when it gets dark very soon.

Q: Right, uh, so you don't sit on the nest like a bird?
A: What do you think? Ridiculous question! I bury the eggs and leave them. They'll hatch in about nine weeks, and the little baby turtles will dig themselves out and run into the sea. It's what I did, right here, about 40 years ago.

Q: Wow, you were born on this beach? Are you sure?

A: Just move that pile of sand, will you? No, there. NO THERE. Of course, I'm sure. All female sea turtles like me remember the beach where we hatched. We return to it when we are ready to become mothers. I had to swim six hundred miles to get here too...

Q: WHAT! Why so far, and how did you find the way? There are no road signs in the ocean–or do you have sat nav?

A: How we find the way is our secret, ha. We travel far to find the best food. I eat delicious sea grass in warm, shallow waters, and also algae, although some BIG BUFFOONS keep dropping this HORRIBLE stuff in the sea that looks like algae but which chokes our guts and makes us ill. GAH!

Q: How annoying. Do you know who they are?

A: Yes. YOU.

Q: Me? I haven't dropped anything in the sea. Except my car keys once. Whoops.

A: I mean HUMANS. You keep throwing PLASTIC BAGS into the water, which look like food to us. And you're BUFFOONS because we get tangled in your fishing nets, caught on your metal hooks, and whacked by your boats.

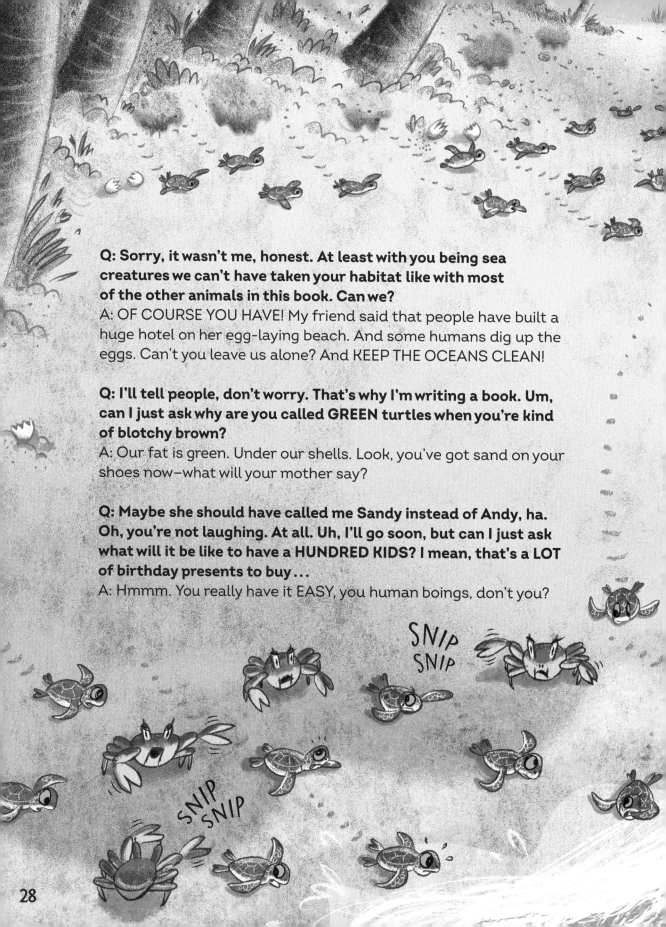

Q: Sorry, it wasn't me, honest. At least with you being sea creatures we can't have taken your habitat like with most of the other animals in this book. Can we?
A: OF COURSE YOU HAVE! My friend said that people have built a huge hotel on her egg-laying beach. And some humans dig up the eggs. Can't you leave us alone? And KEEP THE OCEANS CLEAN!

Q: I'll tell people, don't worry. That's why I'm writing a book. Um, can I just ask why are you called GREEN turtles when you're kind of blotchy brown?
A: Our fat is green. Under our shells. Look, you've got sand on your shoes now—what will your mother say?

Q: Maybe she should have called me Sandy instead of Andy, ha. Oh, you're not laughing. At all. Uh, I'll go soon, but can I just ask what will it be like to have a HUNDRED KIDS? I mean, that's a LOT of birthday presents to buy...
A: Hmmm. You really have it EASY, you human boings, don't you?

SNIP
SNIP

SNIP
SNIP

Q: It's beings, not boings. But what do you mean?
A: I mean, when you're little you don't have enormous MONSTERS just swooping down and eating you, do you? Or beasts with giant claws that grab you and pull you into their dens?

Q: No, that would be no fun. Why do you ask?
A: Because WE DO. When my eggs hatch, whole gangs of big hawks and other hungry birds will swoop down onto the beach and grab my tiny turtles as they flee toward the sea. Or ghost crabs will snatch them. It's a DEADLY DASH. Some will drown in the waves too. Not many survive …

Q: Wow, that's HORRIBLE. No wonder you're endangered. Can we help you at all?
A: Well, actually there are a few NICE HUMANS who do protect our beaches and guard the eggs and our babies. And I heard about others who are trying to stop turtle fishing. So you're not ALL BAD, I suppose …

Q: Whew! Is there anything else you want to tell me?
A: Yes. MOVE OUT OF THE WAY! I want to park my butt in this hole so I can lay some eggs.

29

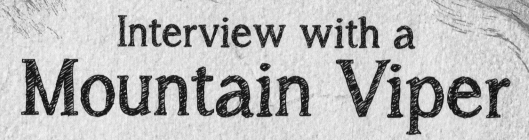

Interview with a
Mountain Viper

Now I come face to face with a dangerous reptile in the high, stony valleys of Turkey. Why am I doing this? I must be NUTS. Here goes...

Q: Um, am I safe being near you?
A: Of course! I am a venomous snake, but I don't want to bite YOU.

Q: Why not? Because I'm nice and friendly?
A: No, it's because you're too big to eat. It would be a TOTAL WASTE of my precious venom. I only eat small creatures that I can swallow whole, like mice and lizards.

Q: Whew, that's a relief! So can you tell me something about yourself?
A: Well, I am a central Turkish mountain viper, and I live here in the dry, rocky mountains of Turkey, but actually I am VERY keen to see more of the world—I want to TRAVEL!

DINNER IS SERVED!

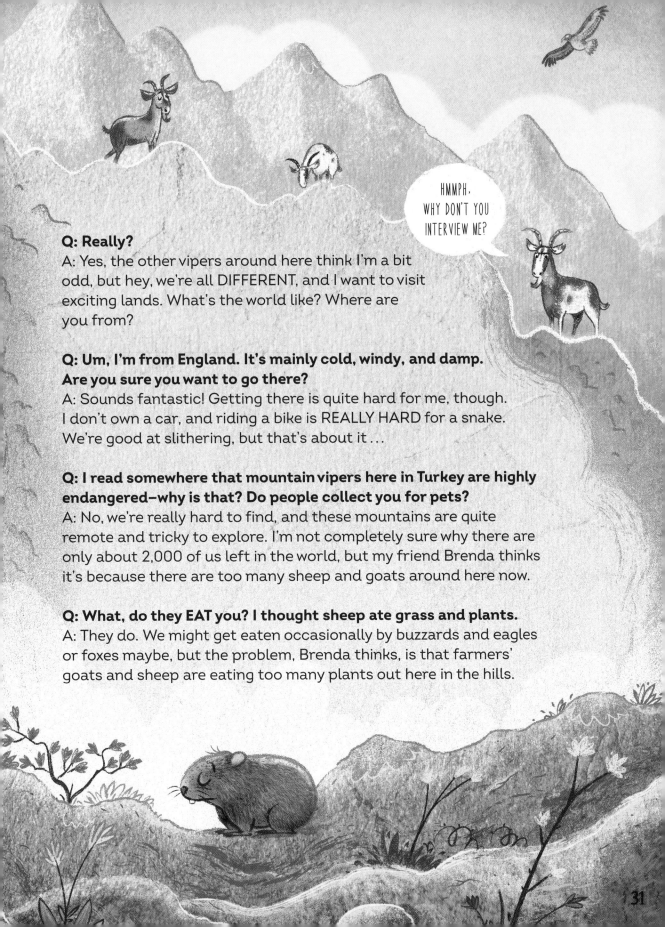

Q: Really?
A: Yes, the other vipers around here think I'm a bit odd, but hey, we're all DIFFERENT, and I want to visit exciting lands. What's the world like? Where are you from?

Q: Um, I'm from England. It's mainly cold, windy, and damp. Are you sure you want to go there?
A: Sounds fantastic! Getting there is quite hard for me, though. I don't own a car, and riding a bike is REALLY HARD for a snake. We're good at slithering, but that's about it …

Q: I read somewhere that mountain vipers here in Turkey are highly endangered—why is that? Do people collect you for pets?
A: No, we're really hard to find, and these mountains are quite remote and tricky to explore. I'm not completely sure why there are only about 2,000 of us left in the world, but my friend Brenda thinks it's because there are too many sheep and goats around here now.

Q: What, do they EAT you? I thought sheep ate grass and plants.
A: They do. We might get eaten occasionally by buzzards and eagles or foxes maybe, but the problem, Brenda thinks, is that farmers' goats and sheep are eating too many plants out here in the hills.

HMMPH, WHY DON'T YOU INTERVIEW ME?

Q: But how does that affect you?
A: That's what I said to Brenda! She said, "Oh come on, it's OBVIOUS. We eat mice and voles, and they eat plants. If there isn't enough food for them, then there won't be so many mice and voles, and it's harder for us to survive, geddit?"

Q: Do you think she's right?
A: I have NO CLUE, I just want to TRAVEL. Have you been to Iceland? It's full of ice! I hear the volcanoes and glaciers are amazing.

Q: No, but I've been to Poland.
A: Was it full of po?

Q: No. Um, can I ask you about the fancy pattern on your scales. What's that about?
A: Brenda says it helps us stay hidden among the rocky places around here—so our prey can't see us, and so predators miss us too, hopefully. It's called camel-something.

FOX AT 10 O'CLOCK, HAWK AT TWO!

Q: Camouflage?
A: Yes, camelflage. Anyway, tell me about the other exciting places you've been. I want to see the bright lights: New York ... Paris ... Tokyo ... Tulsa.

Q: Hopefully you'll get there someday. First can you tell me how you catch your prey?
A: Yes, no problemo. We often keep still and wait for a small mammal or bird to come by, or we sneak up on them. If they are close enough, we open our mouths wide, load up our fangs, and dart forward, giving them a quick bite to inject our deadly venom.

Q: Oh, wow—then what?
A: If it's a mouse or similar, it'll run away but soon die from the poison. Then we just follow its smell, find it, and swallow it whole, yum num!

Q: Right, thank you Mr. Mountain Viper, that's been really interesting, but now I must go.
A: Ooh, ooh, can I come with you? I travel light—I don't have any clothes!

I THOUGHT THEY WERE DUE AT FIVE!

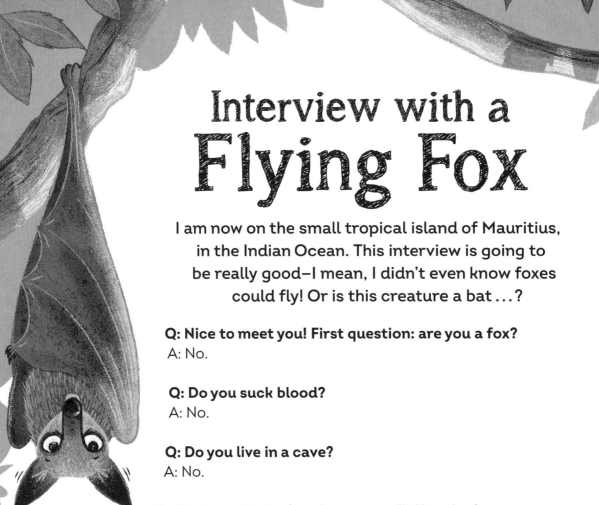

Interview with a
Flying Fox

I am now on the small tropical island of Mauritius, in the Indian Ocean. This interview is going to be really good—I mean, I didn't even know foxes could fly! Or is this creature a bat...?

Q: Nice to meet you! First question: are you a fox?
A: No.

Q: Do you suck blood?
A: No.

Q: Do you live in a cave?
A: No.

Q: Oh dear, this isn't going very well. Um, don't you like my questions?
A: No.

Q: Do you only say "no"?
A: No.

Q: Um, how can I get you to say something else?
A: Well, by asking better questions, OBVIOUSLY! I am a flying fox, but that's actually a kind of large bat. Our faces look a bit like foxes' faces, that's all. And we roost in trees, not caves, and we would never suck blood—that sounds DISGUSTING.

Q: Oh, sorry. Um, what does roost mean?
A: It means to sleep or rest.

Q: But you do hang upside down, right?
A: Of course! We have strong claws to grip the branches. It's easy to take off when you hang like that because you're already up in the air.

Q: So you're not a vampire then?
A: No, mainly because THEY DON'T EXIST.

Q: What about the vampire bats of South America? They drink the blood of animals.
A: Never heard of South America. Anyway, we flying foxes eat fruit—that's why we're fruit bats, see. We also nosh on flowers and leaves and nectar sometimes too. Yum yum.

IF YOU'RE DOWN THERE, DON'T LOOK UP!

Q: Is there much fruit on this island?

A: Well, there used to be lots of rainforest here and plenty of fruit growing on the trees. TONS of it. But SOMEONE keeps chopping down the trees. SOMEONE keeps clearing the land for farming and houses and roads. And growing plants that don't belong here.

Q: What! Total buffoons! Who would– oh. I see. You mean humans, don't you?

A: Yes, YOU PEOPLE. I wish you would just leave us in peace! We can't win! We don't have enough fruit in the rainforest, so sometimes we have to munch the mangos and lychees that the farmers grow. But because we eat their crops, people are now allowed to shoot us with guns!

Q: Oh, that's horrible—no wonder you're endangered. Or are there other reasons too?

A: Yes! We sometimes get big tropical storms here in Mauritius, called cyclones. Those can be deadly for us. It's not like we can fly across the HUGE ocean to live somewhere else . . .

Q: Yikes, OK, let's lighten things up: what's GOOD about being a bat?
A: Oh, lots of things. Our thin, light wings mean we are CHAMPION flyers. And we are the biggest mammal on these islands too. Plus, our POOP helps new forests grow.

Q: What? How?
A: It's full of fruit seeds. When we do a number two in midair, it drops down all over the place and the seeds can grow into new fruit trees.

Q: Wow, that's amazing. We should be doing more to protect you, shouldn't we?
A: EXACTLY! We don't want to end up as dead as a dodo—they used to live here too, you know. So did the giant tortoise.

Q: You mean they're extinct?
A. Exactly. Extinct, IT STINKS!

Interview with a
Nimba Toad

My next conversation takes place high up on a grassy
mountain in Africa. I'm in a country called Liberia,
and I'm talking to a very sassy little amphibian!

Q: Hi! Is it OK if I interview you?
A: What's the deal? What do I get out of it? I bet you get paid
for this while I get NOTHING. How is that fair?

Q: Oh, um, well, do nimba toads use money?
A: No, but that's NOT THE POINT. I seek JUSTICE for toads!

Q: Right. Um, is that because you're very endangered animals?
A: Well, common toads are not endangered, nor cane toads or
natterjacks or golden toads or Texas toads or the giant African
toad or even the oriental fire-bellied toad. But WE ARE.
Yes, there are only a few western Nimba toads like me left
on the planet. I demand CHANGE!

Q: What changes do you want?
A: We DEMAND that dooman beings like you—that's humans who
bring doom—stop making HUGE HOLES on the mountain here
where we live and then squashing the soil down so it's ROCK
HARD. It's ruining our lives!

Q: Why are people making holes here on Mount Nimba?
A: They want to dig iron out of the ground to make big metal things. But they are mining away OUR HOMES. We insist that it stops NOW!

Q: Um, you're asking a lot for someone who's very small, aren't you?
A: Hey, I may be less than an inch long, but we Nimba toads were here long before the noisy diggers and giant bulldozers that ruin our habitat.

Q: Fair point. What was that you said before about them squashing the ground?
A: It's a CRIME! The mining machines are so heavy that they press down the soil so it's hard as rock and we can't dig into it. This must be banned. NOW.

Q: Why do you dig into the soil? To find food?
A: No! This part of West Africa gets very hot in the dry season from November to March. We cannot survive the heat. We need to keep moist, so we bury ourselves underground for months until the rainy season comes.

Q: Right, I see. What do you get up to in the rainy season?
A: Mating. If we don't mate, we don't survive at all as a species.

Q: Ah, OK, so do females like you look for ponds for your eggs, like frogs do with frogspawn?
A: No. We are on a MOUNTAIN, in case you haven't noticed. There are not really any ponds up here, even in the rainy season. We are very unusual toads because we give birth to live babies.

Q: Wow, they must be TEENY TINY. Are they?
A: Yes, about a quarter of an inch. I usually produce around ten toadlets at a time.

NO, YOU'RE TOO YOUNG FOR A BIKE.

JUSTICE FOR TOADLETS!

Q: Whoa, that's a lot of kids to care for—do you have a nanny?
A: No, but that is an excellent idea. I DEMAND nannies for toads! We want change! We want free childcare. And better food. Less mining, more dining!

Q: Well, hopefully this interview will be in a book and lots of people will read it and things might change for the better?
A: I hope so. But I bet I still won't get paid.

Q: I'll have a word with the publishers . . . Um, can I just ask, when you climb out of the ground in April, how do you find a mate?
A: It's not easy. We can't see much in the long grass, so we rely on sound. The males have a mating call that we follow to find them.

Q: OK, what's the call? "Lonely toad here"? "Come for a cuddle"? "Whoopeeeee"?
A: No, it's more of a very faint "bing."

Q: Bing?
A: Yes, WE DEMAND BETTER MATING CALLS! JUSTICE FOR NIMBA TOADS NOW!

Interview with a
Tiger Chameleon

I have now brought the tranimalator to a small tropical island in the Indian Ocean to meet a creature that is, well, like none other on Earth!

Q: Good morning. How are you today, Mrs. Chameleon?
A: PROFESSOR Chameleon to you.

Q: Whoops, sorry, I didn't know that chameleons can be profs.
A: There are clearly a LOT of things you don't know. For example, do you know the name of these islands we live on?

Q: Seychelles?
A: Shells.

Q: Ah, that's a joke, isn't it? Seychelles and "say shells," ha!
A: No, we tree lizards call these the Shell Islands. I do NOT make jokes. I am always DEADLY serious.

Q: Wow, so how do you have fun? Do you swing from the branches? Maybe wear costumes occasionally?
A: Cease your wittering, human nitwit. How can we think about FUN when every day is a matter of LIFE and DEATH? We might not find enough food, we might be grabbed by a snake or hawk, we might fall out of a tree ...

Q: Ah, is that why you're endangered?
A: No, that is primarily due to habitat loss resulting from the introduction of alien vegetation into the forest.

Q: What! ALIENS are getting you? Man, that is BAD. Do they have laser rays and ginormous heads?
A: Hmmm. I am referring to alien PLANTS. Non-native species.

Q: It's getting worse! You're being bashed by TRIFFIDS?
A: Are you sure you're an author? I am talking about trees and bushes that have been PLANTED by people like YOU—crops like cinnamon.

Q: I never did like cinnamon. It ruins apple pie. So, uh, we naughty humans have been cutting down your forests and growing spices where you live?
A: At LAST, you have it. We rely on trees to catch insects like grasshoppers and mantids.

Q: Oh yes, is it true you have a GROSS long, sticky tongue that you can shoot out of your mouth at about 5,000 miles per hour?
A: It's not GROSS, it's clever! Yes, my tongue is longer than my body, and I can fire it toward my prey in one-hundredth of a second. The sticky end uses suction to grab the insect and zip it back into my mouth. But not THAT fast.

Q: Well that sounds like fun! Isn't it?
A: Well, I suppose it's more exciting than hacking at a steak with a blunt fork, yes.

Q: And can you also change color for camouflage?
A: That is a myth. I mean not true. Our skin is able to display different colors, yes, but we do it for communication—to tell rival chameleons to go away, for example, or to attract a mate.

Q: Like a first mate on a ship? Well that sounds adventurous, I didn't know you went on sea voyages.
A: NOT that kind of a mate... HONESTLY! I mean a partner of the opposite sex for the purposes of reproduction. If we don't have children, we really will die out!

Q: Oh, I get it now! Is it true there are only about 2,000 tiger chameleons left in the world?
A: Probably. Possibly. I don't go around counting. But because we live on small islands there is only a limited area of forest for us all to live in.

THIS COLOR MEANS GET LOST!

Q: Right, that's tough. Um, can I ask why you're called a tiger chameleon when you don't have stripes, claws, big teeth, or fur?
A: Well, I am gray-green, but some of us are yellow-orange with black markings, so that's the most likely origin of the name. I certainly don't roar or hunt antelope . . .

Q: And finally, can you tell me why you rock back and forth like that? Are you nervous?
A: No. Annoyed, yes; frustrated, yes; astonished, YES, but not nervous. These actions mimic the movements of branches and leaves in the wind—so predators are less likely to spot us. Of course, it also helps that we can spot them with our 360-degree vision . . .

Q: Ah yes, the swively eyes—they're EPIC! I like your special feet too. Just before I go, is there anything that you want to tell the world?
A: Yes. Be kind to lizards, stop warming the planet, read more books, and don't PICK YOUR NOSE ON THE BUS.

Thank you for the interview, professor!

How you can help

I learned so much from doing those interviews, especially about all the reasons that different animals are endangered. WHAT A MESS we humans have made of caring for some of these amazing creatures!

But WAIT, hope is not lost! There are LOTS of good people in the world who are working hard to PROTECT the animals that most need our help.

Remember too that there are endangered animals in ALL parts of the world. They're not all huge like rhinos or scary like crocodiles—there are butterflies, bees, birds, little newts, and much more that need our help too! Read these ideas and see what YOU can do!

1. See some wildlife
Ask if you can go to a national park, nature reserve, wildlife sanctuary, or zoo:
* See what you can spot
* Learn about local wildlife
* Discover what work is being done to protect animals under threat

2. Raise money
Ask at home if your grown-ups can help you raise some money to give to a nature nonprofit organization that protects wildlife that is under threat.
* Think of something that would be fun to do, such as having a garage sale with old toys or books, or selling yummy bakes you've made
* Ask a teacher if your school can get involved with raising money for wildlife
* Do a challenging outdoor activity for which you collect donation pledges

3. Clean a beach or pick up litter

Litter is harmful to all kinds of wildlife. Trash left on a beach can also be washed out to sea and affect marine life in faraway places. You'll need adults to help you organize this!

🌿 Find out if there is a local voluntary group that does beach cleaning.

🌿 Take a bag each and do a bottle search: use gloves or litter pickers to collect plastic bottles or other plastic waste. Take them for recycling.

🌿 Remember, do not put any trash or plastic collected in trash cans— these can get too full and overflow back into the environment!

4. Speak out

Leaders, bosses, and people in charge have the power to make things better for our planet's wildlife. A good way to get them to think about endangered animals is to write a letter with some ideas for things that they might do. Ask a grown-up who to write to and how to send it!

5. Use less stuff

Making and using things needs energy, and the more energy we use, the more POLLUTION we make. We only have one Earth, and it's home to every living thing, including endangered animals. If lots of people do small things like these, it can make a big change:

🌿 Try not to waste things like water, food, and paper

🌿 Turn off lights and devices when not using them, to use less electricity

🌿 Where possible, choose walking and biking instead of going by car

🌿 Be an avid recycler

🌿 Don't litter

6. Get drastic with plastic

Scientists have discovered that billions of tiny pieces of plastic end up in oceans, rivers, and land. They then get into animals' bodies, sometimes causing harm. NOT NICE.

🌿 Instead of plastic bags, choose any bag that can be reused lots of times

🌿 For drinks, use a bottle that can be refilled, instead of throwaway bottles

🌿 Use bars of soap instead of shampoo and shower gel in plastic bottles

7. Be in the know

One of the very best things you can do is to join your local public library. It's FREE! You can find out more about endangered animals and some of the special projects to protect them. The more we understand, the more we can help.

Quiz

Can you answer these fun questions about each of the ten endangered animals in the book? All the information is on the pages somewhere. Answers are at the bottom of this page.

1. What do black rhinos eat?
a) White rhinos   b) Grass and other plants   c) Antelope   d) Soup

2. How do Cuban crocodiles catch rats?
a) By leaping up out of the water into trees   b) They don't
c) By pretending to be a log   d) With booby traps

3. How do flying foxes help trees grow?
a) By watering them b) By eating weeds   c) By digging holes   d) By pooping in flight

4. What do baby giant pandas look like?
a) Big, black, and white   b) Small, blind, and pink
c) Yellow with purple spots   d) Jolly Ranchers

5. What do nasty poachers kill Sumatran elephants for?
a) Their tusks   b) Their skin
c) To stop them from trampling crops   d) Because they are bullies

6. Why do tiger chameleons change color?
a) To show off   b) For camouflage
c) To attract a mate   d) To reflect jungle fashion

7. What have Nimba toads had their habitats destroyed by?
a) Hikers   b) Mango farmers
c) Mining machines   d) Elvis Presley

8. How many mountain vipers are there left in the world?
a) 6   b) 59,000   c) Four million   d) 2,000

9. What harmful thing do green turtles sometimes mistake for food?
a) Plastic bags   b) Tea bags   c) Handbags   d) Fishing nets

10. What is the loud mating call made by male kākāpō called?
a) Boinging   b) Boogying   c) Booming   d) Brian